D0993219

Midden

Poets Out Loud

Elisabeth Frost, series editor

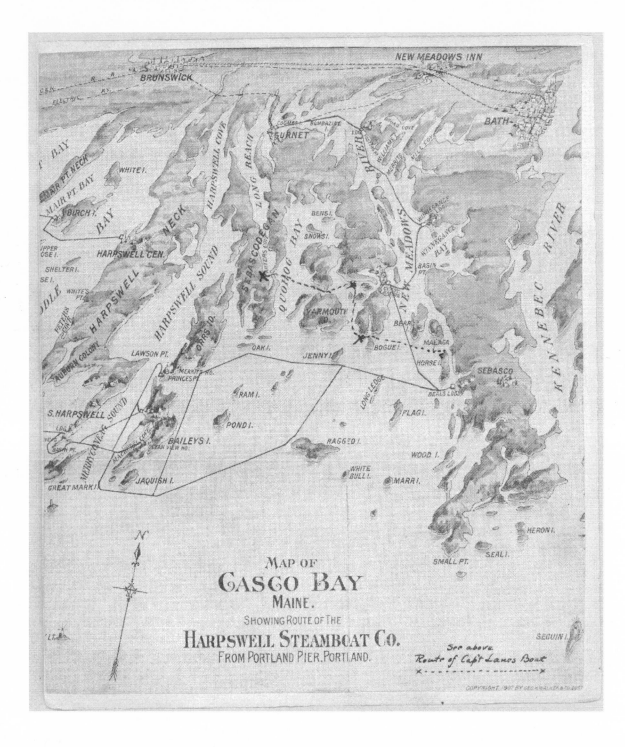

MAP OF
CASCO BAY
MAINE.
SHOWING ROUTE OF THE
HARPSWELL STEAMBOAT CO.
FROM PORTLAND PIER, PORTLAND.

See above
Route of Capt Lanes Boat

Midden

Julia Bouwsma

Fordham University Press New York 2018

Frontispiece: Map of Casco Bay, Maine, *History of Lane's School on Malaga Island*, p. 26, Mss A 1900, R. Stanton Avery Special Collections, New England Historic Genealogicial Society.

Fordham University Press has no responsibility for the persistence or accuracy of URLs for external or third-party Internet websites referred to in this publication and does not guarantee that any content on such websites is, or will remain, accurate or appropriate.

Fordham University Press also publishes its books in a variety of electronic formats. Some content that appears in print may not be available in electronic books.

Visit us online at www.fordhampress.com.

Library of Congress Cataloging-in-Publication Data available online at https://catalog.loc.gov.

Printed in the United States of America

20 19   5 4 3

First edition

For the residents of Malaga Island and their descendants,
and for all our ghosts—

Contents

In 1912 the State of Maine forcibly evicted an interracial community of roughly forty-five people from Malaga Island, a small island off the coast of Phippsburg. Though Malaga had been their home for generations, nine residents (including the entire Marks family) were committed to the Maine School for the Feeble-Minded in Pownal, while the others struggled to find homes on other islands or on the mainland, where they were often unwelcome. The Malaga school was dismantled and rebuilt as a chapel on another island. Seventeen graves were exhumed from the Malaga cemetery, consolidated into five caskets, and reburied at the Maine School for the Feeble-Minded. Just one year after the start of the eviction proceedings, the Malaga community was erased.

Foreword: Midden, When Glory Comes

In the aftermath of a tragedy such as that of the erasure of the culture of "mixed race" people on Maine's Malaga Island, there is the whisper of imagined wind over a midden, the remains of shells and other things tossed into a pile. Then comes the gift of a heart of a poet filled with compassion, building an empathic palette rooted in that compassion, as she creates an appeal to the human heart for a gesture toward some kind of peace and justice. With *Midden*, both stunning and profound, Julia Bouwsma gives us poems that remind us of the capacity for humans to be utterly cruel to one another, as well as hope for greater possibilities for healing, forgiveness, and love.

In choosing *Midden* for the Poets Out Loud Prize, I was impressed with her craft. The book is an assemblage of observations from the present, dialogues with the ghosts of the people whose entire lives were removed so cruelly and violently from their homeland, and interior dialogues of the poet with herself, a multilevel layering of voyages. The book strikes me as a merger of craft and reverence, a brave moving into the space of an otherness to express the deepest concern for justice and for the evocation of a lost beauty. In a word, it is glory.

Bouwsma shows us the horror, in poems that are full, yet marked with a deftness and appropriate concision. Brevity holds the horror until we are ready to receive it in its fullness. The experience of knowing and believing is accomplished by the poet who has first done just the same process of discovery and experiencing the heart stirring to make change.

With Bouwsma's poems, whispers of glory arise for the ghosts and the pain they endured. Let us hope these poems inspire the arrangement of scores of songs to be sung for redemption and another step toward holding the human heart back from tragedy.

Midden is a gift among givers.

—Afaa M. Weaver 尉雅風
West Cornwall, Connecticut
October 12, 2017

Midden

I Walk My Road at Dusk

The hour of metamorphoses, when people half hope, half fear
that a dog will become a wolf
——JEAN GENET, *PRISONER OF LOVE*

Now is the hour between: light dances
animal-eyed among the trees. Every bending
branch becomes a torso. Every mouth opens
into another running tooth, woods stripped
naked as a fleeing child—

what leaps the downed logs, what sudden antlers
clatter the brush heap?

I walk to the clear cut—discarded
limbs, silvered softwood. I trace
this trail of quartz crystals, vertebrae—
morsels dropped from a torn pocket and blazed
to bone dust. The road curves toward
and away. The road spines
the stone walls. My feet stumble inside
ruts my feet have worn.

All I ever wanted was land: something to press
my fingers into, a flat weight to pin my breath
into the sockets of my hips.

What body doesn't hide secrets from itself?
I strain to see the path, stones sleeping in the road
like fallen dogs—

the sun drops its animal rush
into my throat, and I call out

to you, the erased, the in-between,
islanders, whose bodies still wear your moment of dusk
as a skin of rusted dirt you cannot
crawl out of, you

touched and turned, tossed by the phantoms
others saw as they gazed from the mainland, the white eye
of the sun falling into the dark mouth where river
meets ocean, a rupture of self

from self, our otherness a shadow that pitches us into
the blue hour from which there is no escape—
the dog rising from its bed of dust
to take the wolf's heart in its mouth.

The Way Home

Day after day, we broke down the beavers' dam
and day after day they built it back.

It was an endless summer of rain. Water clotted
the road. Water so high they swam

in front of my car as I climbed the long road
to our cabin on the hill.

•

I stood in the road after work, pants rolled
to my knees. The rain poured down.

Dress shoes in one hand, I dragged
the newest branches to the other side—

their chewed points stuck
like spears as I hurled them
into the bog.

•

The second summer we called Fish and Wildlife,
but Fish and Wildlife wouldn't come.

We only trap beavers to kill, they said. *Try to move them,
and they'll just find their way home.*

•

Eventually, my husband shot them, fished
their sodden bodies

from the pond
with the neighbor's kayak.

First the male, skinned hide salted—
we ate the meat with eggs.

It tasted of poplar bark, bitter
swamp.

•

Fall came: the female hung
in our shed, froze before there was time

to skin her out.

I drove the long road home,
no crunch of branches under my car.

•

All winter, I tried to write the island
to life, labored

these voices, the people torn

up, dug
from their land—

all winter, the beaver hung in my shed,

her body frozen and still,
upside down in the dark.

Dear ghosts, I pick the list

for names like herring bones from the fish's
oiled cavity. I run them between my teeth, stroke
the scarred light of photographs—your granulated
faces, mimeographed eyes always left
in the dark. I take up scissors, razor blades, the rusted
garden loppers, pinking shears. I scissor you
to islands, rearrange until my fingerprints peel
your faces gray. I bind you to my walls. I let you
hang. You watch me sleep, your silence a blood-burst
in my mouth. I dream of ink, wake as a stain
against my sheets. Finally I shred the maps, scatter
the portraits, watch you faceless flutter down—
a hundred-year-old snow dusts the ground.
This is our only blessing: bury you in the yard, sing
as I fingernail our forgetting into the bone clay.

The Story of Fire

Our brushfires hung thick and black. They kept
us warm, cooked our pots of clams,
and every day the villagers smelled our smoke
from their porches on the mainland.

A stick on fire curls and curls,
each fiber glows as it peels
from the stalk. So it is with a story,
driftwood flames green to blue:

How they came in boats,
how our shacks caught like a shot of light
when match met kerosene. How we left
in their boats; how we huddled
close; how mama bent
to the baby, her crooked
arm clamping him
silent. How a child curled
mouth to smoky knees and bit
them to red.

A stick on fire—

Now, one hundred years later,
the archaeologists find
no ash, no scorched ground, no scraps
of charred wood, just loose nails
in the shell heap:

evidence that when the villagers said *leave,*

we willingly tore our houses down
with our hands.

Their Objects

medicine bottles   tureen   hatchet   flint   bullets   shotgun shells   straight razor   fishhooks   knife   bone knife handle   clay pipes   buttons   beads Johnson's Liniment bottle   key   jug   bowl   milk pan   cup   drinking glass   nails   fishhooks   box lock   teapot   stove parts   bottle   clay pipe   comb   mug   lamp   chimney-brick   spoon   buttons   beads pipe-bowl   plates   saucers   bottles   milk glass dish   cup   bowls lamp chimneys   lamp handle   door-hinge   fishhooks   rope

Shipwreck at New Meadows

Say the ship swivels and tips   Say the lantern swings
before it shatters

spit of light—

Say a slave watches his master

recoil to his knees
behind the mast

All around them the sea is wet with fury, ravenous
for the clench   Take a breath

and into the snap
they go

this swirl of limbs—
master, slave—

choking on salt   gagging on cold

Say under the water the world is lung-less

and master's braided coat
pulls   him
waterlogged

to a place colder than right
to a mouth that curdles
words

Say   driftwood fingers grope
a floating plank

as this hand grabs wet wool

Bas-Relief: Jake Marks

Beyond his shoulders, bleached sky, hint of
clouds. Behind his head, wrinkled ocean, the rock
on which he stands. Whittle this man, cut him
from his landscape, cut him against it—
they say he feared water but lived on an island.
Here skin, salt cured, ocean hardened,
cracks to cancer. Let sunlight chisel his cheek—
let it leave a patch whiter than clamshells bleached
to the shore. Here are limbs tilted and braced:
in his right hand, a stick (handle to an unknown tool);
his left hand a bulge of veins that crawls
up his wrist. Here an elbow juts, and stains gather
on the bib of his overalls. Carve it: the dark beard
with its specks of white (gray hairs or sea foam),
a strap on one shoulder, open cuffs—
how his hair, caught in the wind, flutters up.

Dear ghosts, in winter my camp on the hill becomes

an island, plowed road over half a mile out. We walk
with pack baskets, snowshoes, a sled to haul the grain. Our tracks
disappear behind us—*how the wind hungers to erase us!* When I say
camp I mean my house has no foundation. We cut a trapdoor
in the floorboards, dig a hole in the earth beneath: jars of pickles
and mincemeat, apples and carrots, potatoes. The mice ransack
our rations, score them with teeth-marks. In the kitchen, fire
belly-churns the cast iron ribs of the cookstove. Wind punches
the front door open, coils around the cabin, braids itself up the woods,
over the mud, skim-ice glinting the ditches. My hill swallows
a neighboring hill. The neighbor's car crawls slowly home, headlights
beaming brighter than a coyote's eye, seeking me out. *The wind
is just a voice inside my head*, I tell myself as the wind breathes back,
as the wind tells itself, tells me. Who will erase the wind? *Enough!*
It doesn't stop. This night is made of all our breath—

Interview with the Dead

Who were you then?

And instantly the tongue becomes the prism
of fracture, land of washed green light—

ferns, wild hops, hemlock, lichen
skinning the granite outcrops.

And instantly the tongue becomes a well—
a stone cast into memory's falling.

When there's no one left to name the helix of departure
unfurling inside you—

wear silence as a tattered shirt, a stain
of torn buttons.

We carried it in our spines
and anyone could see it when we walked.

And instantly the tongue turns to salt,
white film and blanch

for not even the tongue can taste
what came before salt.

How do you remember your island?

As stone fingers spread an octave into the sea

As salt brands ankles and red-mud heels callous to clay

As dreams in which we still pick blackberries

As brambles scratch a map into our skin

As we thread the fishhook, pull the line taut

As a catch of blood in the back of the throat

As fingers tying a knot

How did you leave?

Our houses became our bodies—we lashed
ourselves to rafts. Our bodies became boats.
Some left as cargo in boats, boxes.
We wept or did not weep

until *home* became the rubble
between our teeth: the thing one cannot
bite for fear of breaking.

Then we were a people sculpted of wind,
and when we left, we scattered as breath,
lingered as breath—

then we were a people carved of gravel and dust,
and we left as the land
stripped from the land—

carrying our hearts in our fists.

Where did you go?

To hallways
of sweat and bleach

to white walls and
locked doors

to brass bed frames
and the endless folding of sheets

to the thin lips of strangers
at the market

to back doors
of summer mansions

to mudflats
and shanty camps

to clusters of islands
too tiny to name

to houses rebuilt
with the same old boards

but smaller this time
and the windows

all in the wrong place.

What did you leave behind?

Our arms spread out around it all

until our hands could not
meet our hands.

Dear ghosts, because you tell me to, I begin again

at the body's end—with the discards, the spent, the curled
husks of yesterday's warmth. I scrape the firebox clean. I scrape
the hearth. If it sears, if it's hot, if it's still smoking. I carry you
close, hold you inside whatever part of me continues
to burn. If it's soft as a new scar. If I touch it
and it crumbles. If I touch it and think *heartbreak.* Sift
it to the can, but keep the ashes covered. Keep the ashes
on the back step. You say, *You never know when you'll need
the dead.* The living are papery, split straight, easy
as ash logs. Our grief pops loud as pine, burns
so loose we're gone before we know it. Or we smolder
sweet and dark in our own hot scent. Birch skin peels
from branch, limbs crackle red, recede to black—
some days I unravel so quickly I don't need a match.

So Many Things

Abbie Marks

They say our family fears water; they think I am afraid
to drown. I dig clams from the flats, ocean licking
the rolled ends of my trousers, mud squelching
my toes. I chink the cabin cracks with rags. I gather
the twigs. I split the driftwood logs, fill my skirts
with blackberries. *I am an island on an island—*
I hoard pennies for the doctor (my husband a mess of limbs
since the illness came), row us to shore. A spoonful
of piss in candle flame curdles like cheese
before our eyes. *Kidneys,* the doctor says. *You won't*
live long. The others call us bad luck. I keep
my mouth shut. Even my daughters call me weak. I twist
their coarse hair between my hands, braid it tight, bind
it with strips of rag. I know soon we will be gone. I watch
the governor's face pock disdain, see the pale ladies shiver
and cluster behind. They will come for us. They will take
us to another place. Each night, I pick my way down
to the beach. I stretch my hands to the sea—an expanse
of dark tongues surrounds us. Each morning I rise, mouth
aswirl with bitterness. I reheat the cornbread, I crumble
the salted fish. *So many things they do not know I know—*

The Tray of Spades

Abbie Tripp

> *photography was invented with blood*
> —ED ROBERSON

i.

At six, Abbie knows to stay behind the fence rails,
though she twists up on the corner post, tries
to grow her body bigger, keeps her eyes down:
things you do in front of any strange animal.

Every step of this yard is hers—the hills
her bare-arched feet press into graveled clay
make a map of her flesh, a geography
of peeled sunlight and cedar bark,

but the arm holding the black box
to the white man's eye casts a shadow
over the grass, the daisies, fades
them to flour sack,

as little Pearlie mouths the rail beside her,
peeks out through the stick fence,
and old Annie Parker creaks her chair—

a rhythm Abbie breathes in
like the sound of the sea as she weaves her toes
into the dust, digs in her heels.

She could follow her feet out of this gate, scrabbling
over the rocks and broken shells to the bay.

Instead she braids her palms
to the top of the fence post, elbows bent
to the rails, torn dress falling all around her
loose and streaked as eider wings.

The white man lifts his black box again, says,
Stand still.

ii.

The flashbulb glints one hundred teeth in an open mouth.
The camera is a cracked door anyone can open—

last winter the frost-heaves swelled like a frown
beneath Annie's house, corner posts shifting
until the door wouldn't latch,
and she tied it shut with rope.

Now she pulls Pearlie onto her lap.
Sometimes the restless heat of a child's limbs will keep
the cold out, will hold the ghosts at bay.

Her face is a haze of brush smoke, acrid snap
of pine pitch, lips collecting in creosote pools,
as she glares the camera down—

Annie knows no good ever comes of a mainlander
staring into your open door.

iii.

Afterward, the picture finds its way to Boston,
where it's cropped and stamped.

The postcard: it sells and sells.

THE TRAY OF SPADES, MALAGO ID.
NEW MEADOWS RIVER MAINE

Dear ghosts, my neighbor catches you with her camera

Orbs cluster
like multiplying cells

behind my head   streaks
of light

like scar tissue
in an X-ray

I'm someone else
entirely—

a man   two front teeth
missing   dirty

blond comb-over
wind-worn skin   We slide

the photo into the drawer
face down
          She snaps another

and another
and another

Am I still me?
          I refuse to look

The Schoolteacher Answers the Call

With patience, and the love of Christ constraining me I hope to win them for myself, and I plan to give the best service of which I am capable to these poor black people to whom I believe the Lord has led me.
—EVELYN WOODMAN TO MRS. LANE, 1909

i.

It's not a voice exactly—no words, no white rush,
but something gentler, like the soft comfort of flour
between my fingers, firmness and certainty rising
like dough beneath my kneading hands.

I keep the island inside my mattress,
(the Lanes' yellowed photograph), trace its silhouette
each morning and each night, until I almost feel
the lichen growing on the rocks, almost taste
the salt on my lips.

God, the stitch that threads the fabric of my skin,
I want to sleep clean as a folded pillowcase.

ii.

The dory turns at the harbor, and there they are:
smoke-stained and flapping thin, my little flock.
Waves slap the stern. In my belly is a line twisting
tight. Heaven hold my secret: this fear
has me gut-hooked, God's will
pulls me taut.

iii.

Abbie Tripp twirls as she claps erasers behind the schoolhouse, dances
herself into a tornado of chalk dust and sunbeam
I spy through the open window.

This girl who could not write her own name is alive
with letters now, as if her whole body were an urgent message,
a note she writes and rewrites, filling page after page
with her childish script, with lines of X's and O's.
I watch as she loops her name into the dirt with her big toe,
over and over, until the whole schoolyard bears her mark.

How I long to break from my desk, to link hands with her,
to laugh as the wind catches our skirts!

Instead I turn to tomorrow's lessons.

She must learn to press and starch her dress, to hot-curl
her bangs and braid her buns. She must learn to stand still
and stout as a prize calf. She must learn to bear
her crown of horns.

iv.

Dear winter, now I've gone mad and pace the corners
of my small hut behind the school—an animal scenting storm
under the door crack, sniffing for God.

I talk to the windows. Tell no one my ribcage has opened inside me
like a wind-flung shutter. I stalk the doors. Do not let the children see
my lamplight desire to fling the crusts of stale bread, burn
the needlepoint frame, throw the prayer book to the floor.

Instead I write to Mrs. Lane: *The past winter has been a very trying one for me.*

I pry the last of the potatoes from their frost-lined bucket,
haul water from the spring, scrub this clayed earth
from their frozen skins, watch my fingers swell with cold.
I trace the grit through my teeth with my tongue as I eat.

I make no mention of this new hunger swallowing
its way into my heart, this wave-crash after wave-crash against

the shore of my will until I am hollow as a bone pipe,
smooth-polished and stronger than granite.

Instead I write to Mrs. Lane: *The people whose need is always so great . . .*
I want to answer the call.

Sestina Fragments:

Our Teacher Prays for Bread

. . . whoever believes has eternal life . . .
Your fathers ate the manna in the wilderness, and they died.
—JOHN 6:47–49

Teacher   show us how to   ,
eat   without crumbling   .

        bread   she says   a gift from the
        and we   must
                    , must all   eat   .

Our teacher   her head,
        with hands   someday we will be

        from   hunger that crawls belly to soul,
        sweet salt   will not
            that other world for which we   .

Now   we must chew   ,
        teacher at our side   we
                    cold dried fish

Pencils are sent   women   work for the   ,
            our fingers cramp we will be
            the letters we copywords we

God willing   one day we
        ladies   white houses   pass them
        on glistening china.
                    We love teacher and

        in our heads she is. Aloud we   ,
        sweet hymns, voices pitched to   ,
voices pitched to   , tongues aching for   .

The men the state say we cannot be

       recite in the schoolhouse   we   ,
pass the cups   teacher has taught us to   .

Before teacher   , the land we   ,
but now we sing   our heads back
         for   so much we can   :

       wallpaper   garden seeds   we thank you
       new quilt   scraps   the church ladies ,
a barrel   our Sunday   .

Our teacher says sea air   sours
       and our island world   can be hard   .
       newspapers write   we cannot be   .
           eyes   sad as she
       for our salvation   calls   ,

sometimes we wish we'd never   .

Dear teacher   our voices   with yours as we   the voice
     for   ,   all the times
     rising our throats our fate—we have learned   .

Dear ghosts, I wake wishing my body

could be poured like water into the morning rust pail.
I wake with my dreams still in my mouth. Through the endless pace
of morning chores, I recite your names, carry them in my pocket like a charm
of river stones and coiled hair. This land is fevered and does not sleep.
I beg you, *Teach me to hear this unraveling of skin.* I ask too loudly.
Past the stone wall, children's bodies curl to smallness beneath the earth.
I split the hollowed logs, watch the black ants spray the splitter blade then scatter—
your silence is the story shucked from its hull, a dangling red jewel.
The beaver bleeds and bleeds in the barn. Blood freezes its mouth shut.
All day I expect your bones to appear in my basket.

No Man's Land

Governor Plaisted and Council Visit Malaga, July 14, 1911,
as told by Frances Gullifer, his wife

At dawn, the hard-stepped stride of polished boots
on granite ledge as the sloop unloads. We cross
the rock, and the shacks rise
into our gaze, weathered boards rasping
salt gusts. The Governor paces into the wind,
adjusts his hat, does not look back at me.

We ladies know why we're here—we cluster
like gulls, whisper in hushed tones, blush
as our husbands strut the row of battered shanties,
each unpainted door they throw open
with a bang.

A yellow dog scratches for scraps,
hens cobbling beside him unaware.
A tall dark woman scowls from her doorway,
a frizzy-haired child clinging her skirts.

Gustavus's wife tells me she can't believe I wore white
to this No Man's Land. The other black bonnets agree:
I am the only one not dressed for a funeral.

At the schoolhouse, the children are all
round eyes, fastened smiles. Pressed
into blouses for inspection. They open
their mouths in song.

The Governor recites on the necessities of moral living,
bloat-red, spit flecking his mouth, as he preaches.
I stare at the horizon of my husband's neck
until the nausea rises, avert
my gaze.

On the boat ride back, he will bellow
over the breeze—puffed, ruffled breast huffing
to the other men:

The best plan would be to burn the shacks down
with all their filth

I will stare back at the land, little skirts slipping
between the spruce trees, my husband's words
drifting out on the wind—

conditions there   not credible

to the state

the children's silent watching will follow us
as the sloop turns the bend.

And we ought not to have such things
near our front door . . .

Later we return to the hotel in Bath, change
for the theater. I peel out of my white dress
now stained with dust to see

a ring of mud that will never
wash out of the hem.

Annie in the Boat

Annie Parker

The rope's come snapped—I'm cut
from the mooring line

disappearing at last in silence's shawl

this crocheted fog I wrap
close to my breast

just one tear as he dips his oar in
just one soft stroke of finger to cheek

he dips his oar in
one drop of salt to salt sea

then I'll leave as quiet as I lived

Dear ghosts, how can we stop the sunlight spinning the story

from our hands? The boards were pried off one by one, but the threat of fire
will linger under anyone's tongue. Who doesn't carry their own erasures
silently in their spines, limbs horizoned to the past? My old dog shreds
herself a nest in the old quilt, and I Franken-stitch it back up, stumble
the knot. If placed in a room together, you would not recognize the ones
you have become, nor would they recognize you. Too often the poem's fingers
are clumsy with distance, grief the long thread I fail again to tie.
Would it matter if I told you of my own ancestors? Bodies packed
in cattle cars, bodies prodded into dividing lines, the gloved hands that choose
another's fate. Goose-flesh skin surrendered to the clutch of shower tiles,
the final dark release of their bodies coiled into air. All I know is this:
even before I was born I breathed a loss not my own.

John Eason Stops Preaching

One time I slid from a ladder. When I hit ground

my breath arced out of me
vertebrae wheezed
teeth punched right through.

Today the nails are backwards screaming:

split boards pop and fall
in a heap
beside my un-building.

Ever suck in a great gulp of air on a fifteen-below night?

It'll burn a hole right through your lung
leave you doubled up gasping, spitting blood
on the barn floor.

The Lord left me today—

all those years inside my
body like my breath was his house.

This Is Our Home Now

Mr. Pease whistles as he whips the horses up the hill. Wrought
iron twists the dusk—demon forms rising up,
as if from Mrs. Woodman's tattered Sunday book. Like horses,
we do as we're told. We are old enough to smell fear
in our mother's sweat. There are women
in white to meet us, men in white to take
father/brother/son away. There's the strip down:

the icy water spray, the strange coarse clothes—
gray cloth worries our skin. Spit flecks at the corners
of mouths. Down the hall we follow
the punched in faces, follow the narrow backs
into the sleeping room, waxed and wide. We stare
at the bright white sea, at wave after wave of beds.

Sucker Fish

Lizzie Marks

My baby was a sucker fish right from the start: a fat slap and slurp, a thrash
in the net of my belly (and how thin, how patched the net) that summer
I stumbled so full of him each morning down to the shore, nausea a thundercloud
about to split as I heaved into the ocean, jacksmelts gathering to bite my toes,
puked last night's potato scraps into the sea drooling, lifted my skirts
not caring who could see and thought to myself, *Lizzie you've got yourself a sucker fish*
inside of you—he'll eat you whole if it's the only way out. Thick foot hard in the gut,
and I thought, *He's a fighter sure as dawn.* And how happy I was then, knowing
my baby would fight, even with a hook in his gape-hungry jaws. Yes, and he came
out like that too, flopping and red, latched straight on with his fleshy lips—
till that day they drove us from our house, loaded us into the boats, the carriage,
steered us into the bleach cold hall said, *Women go left men go right.* Then I knew the line
was about to snap. A pair of white hands plucked him off my breast. I sagged down
torn, unfurled, gill-slit. And my sweet William he just puckered his mouth.

What William Marks Knows, Age 3

Hunger and the scent of white cloth and all
the cold smells:

windowpane
tile floor
stone wall
changing
table, disinfectant
tin cup, spoon
milk
        (which used to be
        skin-sweet and warm
        but isn't
        now)

porridge
and hands, new hands—they lift
him up

hold him   sack of limbs   little potato head
little onion skin.

The arms are stiff.

The woman they belong to never sings.

Dear ghosts, with a red pencil I draw a map.

With a penknife I carve a wilderness of small cuts. Blood is a road—
the river we carry inside our skins. *The dead are right beside you,*
you tell me, *but you will travel years to find them.* What if every step I take
is a ruin, a heel-dug grave in the crusted snow, a mouth of white?
The stones shift without warning, change shape in the bonelight.
The road stretches through the still-bare trees until I see it turn belly up, glinting.
Even the dog feels it and howls. *In a small clearing, in the heart of the forest,*
your name means nothing, you warn. I vow to start over, promise to get this right.
But each time I begin again by tracing the blank page of my own flesh.

Each Morning Drowns in Open Air

If you could kick your feet through loose shells now, you'd hear
them skitter—the sound of your body forgetting

your body, forgetting your land. Without harbor, longing piles
your skin. Without harbor, cells cluster to islands inside you, white

as bone-bleached sun. You become a terrain for fever, a toothache
in the mouths of strangers as you pass. Without memory,

you become a permeable scent wafting through an empty
hallway, oil soap and wax. One has only to exhale

and you might disappear. If you paused by the mirror
you'd see the fish scales falling from your eyes,

but you never do. To try to name yourself now is to cauterize
an abscess that drains into the heart. Silence is a muscle

you open, then close—practice like sleeping
or eating or prayer.

The Procedure

Lizzie Marks

And then one night a white arm points you
from the supper line back to the room
of starched beds. Before six o'clock rise, they
come for you. They lead you away. A white sheet,
a white towel: you've heard the whispers, how the scent
of ammonia drapes the surgery room. *Be a good girl,*
they say, but you are no longer a girl, and this is not
a question. The bed is wheels and straps, the ether rag
drops, voices *wa-wa-wa*, and all the edges blur
from the walls. The scream is not your own.
Later, back in a body they tell you is yours, breath
sears you to belly. After they untie your arms,
you finger the red seam. The pain hisses out—you
brush your wrists against coarse stitches,
the loose ends of the fishing line.

Upon Opening Another Folded Day

Once an island grew inside you—firm knot
of earth made flesh—

now only the keening of dust on hardwood, the pried-off
lock, the empty rectangle on the closet shelf
where the treasure box used to rest.

Each morning the dream slips anew, so much seawater
between your fingers—

inside the carved hollow of the box, pages curl their empty bodies,
yellow themselves until they are translucent as snakeskin.
Here, a crumpled photograph, a child's record of penciled X's,
a scallop shell small as your toenail, a ring
of pressed and twisted foil.

How you got here is anyone's guess, but surely these
are your memories.

See how the maplewood burl splits a dark mouth.
See how neatly your thumb fits the gap.

Feeble-Minded

Abbie Marks

My heart grows tall as a granite house. Stone to the top,
corridor over corridor over corridor, and me—
a hollowed-out candle left burning in the front hall.
Home, the late-night guest who never arrives. Hear the whisper
like floor drapes I sweep the dust behind: *There are places
for people like you.* I've been here so long my mind
is a lost room: boot-squeak and bleach, rusted latch sticking
the trapdoor. *Memory*, a scrap of cotton I fold and fold
until the fabric strips the scent from my palms. If I don't
make it out, tell my daughters their mother's skin
is an abandoned shed, grayed pine and dry rot, but inside—
inside holds the taste of salt cod, the sweet clotting of blueberries
drying on tin-roof sun. Tell them to jimmy the lock, to search
if they can. Their fingers will remember. Tell them,
Find it. I still have the map.

Dear ghosts, because you are dead and restless

you leer at me from the darkened tree line, howl from the closet
with no door. In the calf-high grass below the garden, the red lines
of your questions harrow me to my knees. Where are the words
for the fact of your once flesh, for your missing? I plunge knuckles
into damp soil, plant the pear tree, tear the old porch boards,
force a pinnacle of blood from the nail-hole in the ball of my foot.
How does it feel to touch? you taunt. *How does it feel to own, to lose, to bleed?*
Your laughter is a water glass breaking between my hands in the sink—
sudden invisible fracture, slow splinter working its way under.
Is this what it means to descend? Stories cut straps into your flesh,
burrow your skin with welts. But if you erase a story—
if I press my arms tight to the doorframe, then step away—
my arms will try to fly from my body.

Lottie Marks Dreams Escape

Around three times like a tornado, scatter myself empty
as a torn dress in summer wind. Now this whole roll
of green hill is the sea and running is swimming through
uncut hay sweet as a kelp stretch. Once I'm gone nothing
will stop me, not bare feet stubbed bleeding nor my sweat
speckled like sea spray and lungs will feel no sting,
will be full luffing sails in the breeze—every acre
I cross a pearl in my mouth. Once I'm gone every sky
will shimmer like a flung match over water. Goodbye land
of gray—ice soak baths wet canvas mouth strapped
belt swinging like a black snake, gone. Already
I feel the sun braising my face. Witchy grass, tell it to me
in a dream. *Soon, soon the backs of my legs will remember you.*

Dear ghosts, there was a man who lived here

before me. Neighbors still call him *Crazy Indian*, say
he liked to walk the road shooting stumps, plastic pint
of Seagram's Seven at his breast, say that he kept
a woman here—round as a tin pie plate, empty
as a bullet hole. That after she left, he filled the house
with coon cats: cats on every counter, every table—
eyes like scorch marks under the wood stove. They say
he raised a field of pot plants out on the front lawn,
a seven-sided pole barn filled with seven years of trash.
The neighbors, they burned it down, but every spring
a shoe or vase burrows from the ground. Beer cans, the sleeve
of an old checked shirt. A baby diaper cut open, caught
in the blades as I mow the grass. He's in jail now, they say,
for all those pot plants. House foreclosed. He left
a loaded shotgun on the table, pointing at the door,
a cold cup of coffee, a tattered photo of his favorite cat.

Lottie Marks on Silence

There is a thing called force of will.
Some have it and some don't.
My father, my brother, my sisters never did,
but I do.

When the newspaper says I don't remember
going to that place, you had best believe
I don't remember.

I can shuck a clam faster than you can blink
an eye. I can tear most anything open.
But not this. This

is the clam you find
at the bottom of the pot—the one still
shut tight. Anybody who knows anything knows
you throw that clam out.

Agent Pease's Defense

It was just math. They asked. The State. So I worked. The figures. Every person has a cost. Every person. Has a price. Divide and subtract. Which to. Commit. Place. Buy out. Order to leave. I was just carrying out. Orders. From the State. And they weren't. Real people. You know. Not like you and me. Ducked their heads. Wouldn't meet our eyes. Couldn't tell. What they were thinking. If they were thinking. Like children. Yes-sir. No-sir. You've got to. Be firm. No use. Feeling pity. I did what was asked. At the end of the day. It was just numbers. It was just math.

Suggestions made by Agent Pease.

State should own island. It could then prevent people from settling there, and turn off the undesirable ones.

What could be done under this condition.

Order Gomez family to Phippsburg,	5
Order Nelson McKenney and family to Harpswell,	7
Buy out James McKenney, Jr., who would probably sell his place for $100.00 and leave the island,	4
Order Jerry Murphy and family to leave. He has stated that he would go when ordered, but it might be necessary to pay him a little, probably $100.00,	6
Order William Griffin and Geo. Marks to leave the island. William Griffin has a house that probably cost $35.00, which might have to be paid for,	2
Place Mrs. Annie Parker in the home for feeble minded. She is a fit subject,	1
Commit Sadie Johnson to Bath Military and Naval Orphan Asylum,	1
Order Eliza and Emery Griffin from the island. They can get a living anywhere,	2
Commit Lottie, Lizzie and James Marks to the home for feeble minded, fit subjects,	3
Send Lizzie Marks child, 2½ years old, to Mrs. Hunt, at Portland. She wants the child,	1
	32

By this disposition, 32 people would be removed from the island.

Midden

Coiled umbilical of a dried daisy petal, toenail
shell, pilfered spoon, three teeth left
in a weasel's yellowed jawbone, rusty fishhook
still lucky, scratch of granite you chiseled
from the wishing rock, words
white as bones never buried in earth—

for every sorrow that's been dug from you,
here is a pile of rubble twice as high.

Dear ghosts, when I said all I ever wanted was land

I meant a body no one could steal. I crumble a clot of earth
between my fingers and my fingers crumble with it, cell by cell.
There you go again, you growl, *leaving pieces of yourself in the road*.
Let them fall. I dig this ground until it furrows a map of my own body
curling or splayed, silent spine of stones laid to rest in the path,
stony hips pointing toward the moon. With each step, let me trample
myself back into myself until there is no room for breath
between grains of dirt, no hollow left. Always, I hear you loudest
in darkness. Night thickens across my skin, and mouths open up
everywhere. A cobweb clings. I swipe and swipe—my arms, my face—
but it won't come loose. You have burrowed a fever under my skin,
become a whisper inside my flesh—like waking from blackout,
like waking still drunk in a tangle of strange sheets. Each day,
you leave your mark—pile of granite at the base of the driveway,
bracelet of bruises blooming my wrists, blood blister
in the toe of my boot. Because of you I am learning to pray:
Let my land become that which no one can enter.
Let my land become that from which I cannot escape.
It was someone else's before mine, but now it is mine—
let me build something, anything, that will last.

Yellow Surprise

Leftover boards whiten on the rocks, dark mounds
of square nails you step around like anthills.
Go to the clearing. The boss will point to the spot: *Dig.*
Cut through moss, hack out roots. Sink your shovel
till the blade stumbles. When you hit flesh, you will hesitate.
You don't want to hurt the dead any more than you've been paid to.
Now scrape the dirt back, the side of your hand thick and wet
among the roots. Hoist her out. She will be heavy as a ballad, limp
arms long as a scream. Maggots eat the mouth out
when you've been under a while. Her lower lip will droop
down to her chin, upper lip lift straight up to her nose.
Bare your teeth with her. Howl in yellow surprise at the sun.

How to Build a Houseboat

Lay the scavenged boards
across
your old scow,

hammer
them tight.

Don't bend the nails too badly—

you must
carry
the next storm,

the old sail
through the trees

so your wife
can keep

alive.

You must
        build

your shack
over again

—only smaller this time—

you are houseboaters now,

always ready

for the scowl
that means *leave*.

Shed Night

Children of Harold Tripp

Daddy's fists you know they're tight as oarlocks and when he gets mad
they silver like cedar knuckle-thick skin peeling back fast
as that chair splinters fast as the bottle rolls
mama steps to the latch we are following the whites of her eyes
daddy is gone to the gale again he is rowing all alone
in an ocean swelling fever like a dead mother's skin
now the back window pull pull little sister cause it's a shed night
sure as dawn will come cracking light under the door
we will hunch all night through the rattle and shake
waiting for the silence that always rolls in before birdsong
time to tiptoe back over these are the pieces and these are his limbs

Potter's Field

Harold Tripp

When Papa finally comes for me, lantern swinging,
snow breaking beneath his boots, I'm flat on my stomach
in the dory, old gray blanket pulled over my head—
fried onions and molasses and scent of sweat.

The doctor asked the town man, *Where to?*
Then the splat of spit as they carried her out.

Now the storm has passed. The dory rocks gently
rocks me steady as Mama's arms—
and a field of long grass, that's what I want
it to be, grass green as the sea in sunshine, dancing
the red bellies of poppies.

Lennie melted a bucket of snow in the cast iron pot. I kept
the fire fed a day and a night, houseboat rattling on its ties,
wind nearly drowning the hiss of her breath.
We took turns wiping the fever back.

Papa hoists me from the dory easy as hauling up a lobster trap,
whispers into the top of my head, *I rowed as fast
as I could, son, fast as I could.*

But I'm past speech. No words will ever
warm this cold in me.

Dear ghosts, you say all our bones are made of paper

so I tear the pages and scatter them to the road. The bones
of my mother's family lie in pretty pine boxes in Hastings-on-Hudson,
near Gershwin's granite tomb. I have been there four times.
I cast my shovelful of earth onto the dead. Each of us did.
Earth is blessing. It holds our stories close in its dark grip, eats them,
yes, but slowly, tenderly. My other ancestors' bones were stacked
neat as cordwood into ovens—they hang above us now—
tethered forever as ash woven into a distant sky. I take
to the woods road each night. I am tattered from walking
so long to find you, from digging beneath this capsized land.
What to fear more: the silence above my head or the silence
beneath my feet? When I whisper the truth, I feel that rush of air
between my ribs, the same as when I tell a lie: the sudden chill
my words strike into your imagined skin. Parched, we chew ice
until horizon spills out of our mouths, stains our lips blue.
All winter the leaky rowboat lies breached on the rocks.
Between the ground and the falling snow, a shard of absence
sharpens itself. Wind salts our throats, the jaundiced sky.

Paddling the Storm

Robert Tripp

Snow on salt water is not erasure—it's jelly, like hog fat
scumming the pot, bobbing below the surface until it becomes
the surface. Dip the oar in, and it clings: memory,
its shoulder-strung rhythm of panic. He's always known
he'd never arrive in time. Between strokes he drinks
this knowledge in. Great gulps salt-sear his throat—
night mouth of wind and sleet, fever crusting like brine
on his dying wife's skin, slow leak in the bottom
of the boat. History is just the moment that won't
let go, body suspended in a motion it can't escape. He lifts
his shoulders, plunges the oars in again and again.

Even after Laura's limbs have stiffened like oarlocks
beneath the sheet, even after he himself is dead
and gone, and his sons and his sons' sons too,
loss steadies itself above the prow constant as the North Star,
loss splinters into the palms of our hands, and behind the dory
slow water still curdles too thick for erasure—
and there's nothing left to do but row and row and row.

Descendant's Riddle

What you don't know could build an island.

What I don't know could fill the sea.

Untold

History cracks our spines like green pine in sun until there's
no need for words, no need to tell the children. *Little Black Foot*, we say,
don't go stirring up trouble. Some things are better left unsaid. And one by one,
names just disappear, laid to rest on mainland granite, the cemetery adjacent
the pits where men shoot cans and ATVs carve circles in soft sand.
One by one, spellings change: The thin stiff posture of "i" softens
and swells to "e," bloating like a worm on a hook, waterlogged and curling
into itself. A "t" surfaces—bony outcrop at the edge of the shoal—
then ducks its head again, silent beneath the breakers. Each day
the lobster traps still need hauling—pull the lines, raise the nets,
slap dinner on the table. Each day we work our hands down
to wet rope and braided coil, don our Carhartt jackets, our salt tongues.
We stay so busy we hardly notice. The century swells its flotsam to the waves.

Dear ghosts, this land harvests the body to rubble.

I slice my spade into it, crawl along the damp rows, squeeze seeds
into its clotted mouth until my knees bleed dirt, until mud splits
my palms like a river delta. Count the stones shrouded with saplings
behind the rusted cemetery gate—the firstborn of this land. Their hands
are rotted to nothing now. Soak beans in a paper cup. Watch
their blanched skins peel to yellow, water-damaged as the pages
of an old genealogy book. I bend to my work. I rake this hungry
earth until my footsteps disappear. Faint green tendrils twist
out of the leaf rot to whisper in my ear: *This is what it means to arrive.*

Erasure

After Holman Day

is   another.
          Between

the sea
                              a trail

                         they have hidden
themselves in the deep
                                        or
                    flood-tide.

Alone—

     ocean creeps   the doors
          and   winter waves thunder

          the din of the sea
     into the head.

Even the
          farmer who sells
                              or takes
does not understand

          the lonely
                    have chosen
          no roads—

The islands

abandoned.

They do not   they do not.

So close,

that stretch of water—

Saudade

who left the sea for the land
who were not welcome on the land

who built of rubble our houses left
on the land our houses left

who were the sticks and stones bruised
bodies dirt to wind

who were the gully who were a scattering
of shells the throat of silenced earth

who were the rubble who dug
the rubble built by bodies left

who left the sea for the land
who let the ocean wash us out

Final Invocation for Ghosts

If I lose myself sinew and marrow
to the furrow, rake, and maul

if year by year my fingers bind as stones
beneath the hardening dirt

if the maple root grows collarbones
if the dogs hear the snow falling and growl at the door

I will become nothing but my steps
ground so cold they leave no trace

let me wipe the ice from the blade
and begin again

each spring the soil weeps, everything shifts a little
my ribs swell green until they crack—

I dig the garden plot, uncover the rusted ties
the rotten scrap-metal every set of hands leaves behind

if I can't scratch through, let me sift the remains
let me carry this shard of you

under my tongue
it will worry a hole

let me swallow

then palms flat to the gravel
together we will name every limb

we will say:

Take hold of your bones
these are your bones.

Afterword

The story of the Malaga Island eviction is not a single story but a tangle of interweaving and knotted and sometimes wholly severed threads. It found me first in bits and fragments: an anecdote my father-in-law told me about meeting a Malaga Island descendant named Justeven in a Lewiston, Maine, bookstore, a ten-minute Maine Public Television video I happened to flip across one late night, a photocopied and now tattered collection of 1900s news articles given to me by someone (I can no longer remember who) more than ten years ago, a series of blurry black-and-white images that I couldn't get out of my mind.

My research has been a poet's research—circular and sometimes scattered but obsessive. I have traveled to the island of Malaga (both independently and on a June 2007 Maine Coast Heritage Trust trip led by Professors Nathan Hamilton and Robert Sanford and students of the University of Southern Maine Archaeology Field School) to the New Gloucester Cemetery, to the Phippsburg Library, to the Maine State Museum, and to the Maine Historical Society. I have listened to numerous audio interviews, thumbed through photographs and letters, studied artifacts, spoken to descendants, and, of course, read many articles and books.

I am grateful to the authors of so many books and articles, all of which have, in some way, informed the writing of this one. Though this is likely an incomplete list, indispensable titles include William David Barry's article "The Shameful Story of Malaga Island" (*Down East Magazine*, 1980); Holman Day's article "The Queer Folk of the Maine Coast" (*Harper's Magazine*, 1909) and his novel *King Spruce*; Nathan Hamilton and Robert Sanford's *Everyday Lives: An Interim Report on Archaeological and Environmental Investigations of Malaga Island, Phippsburg, Maine*; Richard S. Kimball's *Pineland's Past: The First One Hundred Years*; Burke O. Long's essay "The Children of Malaga Island"; Katherine McBrien's *Malaga Island, Fragmented Lives*; Steve Mitchell's *The Shame of Maine: The Forced Eviction of Malaga Island* and *The Shame of Maine: Malaga—The Story Behind the Words*; John Mosher's *No Greater Abomination: Ethnicity, Class, and Power Relations on Malaga Island, Maine, 1880–1912*; Steven T. Murphy's *Voices of Pineland: Eugenics, Social Reform, and the Legacy of "Feeblemindedness" in Maine*; H. H. Price and Gerald E. Talbot's *Maine's Visible Black History: The First Chronicle of Its People*; Franklin Russell's *The Secret Islands*; Lauret Savoy's *Trace: Memory, History, Race, and the American Landscape*; and Celia Thaxter's *Among the Isles of Shoals*.

Additional sources include the Maine State Museum's 2012 exhibit, *Malaga Island, Fragmented Lives;* the 2012 C-SPAN video, *The Evictions of Malaga Island, Maine;* Maine Public Television's 2006 video, *The Story of Malaga Island;* and *Malaga Island: A Story Best Left Untold,* a radio and photo documentary produced by the photographer Kate Philbrick and the radio producer Rob Rosenthal in collaboration with WMPG-FM and the Salt Institute for Documentary Studies.

I am also deeply indebted to those poets whose works have provided me with particular guidance toward this project: Gwendolyn Brooks, Molly McCully Brown, Christian Campbell, Martha Collins, Nicole Cooley, Camille T. Dungy, Claudia Emerson, Tarfia Faizullah, Carolyn Forché, Vievee Francis, Aracelis Girmay, Monica A. Hand, Roxane Beth Johnson, Robin Coste Lewis, Shane McCrae, Mariko Nagai, Patricia Smith, Jean Toomer, Claudia Rankine, Natasha Tretheway, Jake Adam York, C. D. Wright, and Richard Wright. This list, too, is likely incomplete.

For me, the process of researching Malaga has been akin to walking the same road day after day for years, only to stumble over some new remnant or sinkhole each time. To study Malaga is to wonder, continually, if the ground you are walking upon is really what you think it is.

Each time I thought I knew the whole story—each time I thought I had connected the trails of names and dates—I would come across an inconsistency: a date or name or spelling that didn't add up, a contradictory story, a new person I couldn't account for, a family who seemed to have disappeared from the documents without a trace, some sentence I recalled reading but couldn't locate when I went back to confirm it. Part of this is simply the nature of island life in the early 1900s, which could often be itinerant. Part of it is likely incomplete record taking. Much of it is the silence built on decades and generations of shame.

My sense of uncertainty with regard to what I really know about Malaga has stuck with me no matter how much research I have compiled and throughout each draft of this work. By now I know that this sense of uncertainty will stay with me into the book's final stages of production and even as it makes its way into the world—that I will be contacted with facts or stories I have never heard before, with different versions of stories, spellings, and dates, with the potential for error. Poets, by nature, become resigned to the incompleteness of their work, and I am thankful for any new information I may receive, however it finds its way to me.

My land on Millay Hill, in the mountains of western Maine—where many of these poems were begun, miles from the coast and from Malaga—is home to a small cemetery. Here, beyond the rusted and bent fence, lie the bodies of those who found this hillside in the early 1800s and started the slow work of cutting trees, clearing fields, building stone walls, digging wells, building structures, and sowing crops. They claimed the land; they shaped it. And over time, the land shaped and eventually claimed them too.

The cemetery had fallen into disrepair by the time my partner and I came to this property ten years ago. Saplings sprouted wildly, and some full-sized trees had grown up as well. Several headstones had broken off their concrete bases and had either been moved or buried in a thick layer of rotten leaf matter. A large ash had fallen in one corner, knocking down both the fence and the oldest stone.

When I first saw the cemetery, I was filled with awe for the ancestors of my land. But along with awe came uneasiness, perhaps even fear. I wanted to honor these dead by clearing the saplings, cutting the fallen tree, mending the stones and returning them to their proper places. Yet it seemed impossible to do this without also causing disruption. I felt stuck. I didn't want to disturb the dead. But I didn't want to dishonor them by neglecting them either.

I stalled. I made promises to get to work on the project, but I made excuses too. I knew my neglect was disrespectful, was dishonoring the dead of my land. But I feared that acting was disrespectful as well. Shame took over. I walked by the cemetery less often. I told fewer people about it.

Silence has a way of breeding silence.

Eventually you have to break the silence. Even if doing so means disrupting, disturbing the peace, risking anger or sorrow.

Eventually we returned to the cemetery with loppers and saws and got to work. I felt uneasy as we worked. I worried about where to place my feet as I cut saplings— afraid to walk on the dead, unable to complete the task at hand without doing so. I was uneasy, but as we worked, the shame began to lift.

I tell this story because the sense of uneasiness with which I faced the cemetery on my property is so similar to the sense of uneasiness with which I faced the writing of *Midden*.

This book was something I felt compelled beyond reason to write, but I couldn't write it without opening silences and wounds, without causing discomfort and pain, without taking the risk that I might be stepping upon the dead even as I tried to honor them.

I have sought to write into my sense of uncertainty, and though the poems emerge from research, there are numerous places where my imagination has filled the gaps. I have questioned, again and again, my right to tell this story, and I have sought to write into my questions and my doubts. I have sought to write equally into both the horror of silence and the horror of fact.

I can say only that these poems are meant to live in the space between what is known and what is unknown—to speak both of the place from which they come and of the distance from which they were written.

This book is only my version. I am grateful to cast it to the midden of work that has engaged the story of Malaga and its community, and I look forward to watching the mound grow.

Julia Bouwsma
October 2017

Notes

"I Walk My Road at Dusk"

The Jean Genet quote used as an epigraph for this poem is a portion of the epigraph from Christian Campbell's collection, *Running the Dusk* (Peepal Tree, 2010).

"The Way Home"

This poem includes a line that nods to a line from Lesle Lewis's poem "Bear Questions," published in her collection *lie down too* (Alice James Books, 2011).

"Shipwrecked at New Meadows"

Many of the residents of Malaga Island descended from Benjamin Darling, who was said to have been the slave of a Captain Darling. According to one legend, Benjamin Darling saved his master in a shipwreck and was subsequently granted freedom. He married Sara Proverbs and settled on nearby Horse Island.

"Bas-Relief: Jake Marks"

This poem is based on a photograph of Jake Marks. Though I have been unable to verify the original date and source of the photograph, it appeared in a 2011 issue of the *Coastal Journal*, accompanying the article, "Malaga Island History Revisited as Descendants Gather."

"Dear ghosts, in winter my camp on the hill becomes"

This poem pulls language from an earlier poem, "Always a Mouth Wider than My Own," which appeared in my first book, *Work by Bloodlight* (Cider Press Review, 2017).

"The Tray of Spades"

This poem is after a postcard titled *The Tray* [sic] *of Spades* (c. 1907, Boston Post-Card Co.). The postcard was cropped from the original photograph and retitled. The image depicts Annie Parker holding Pearl Tripp on her lap, as her older sister, Abbie, stands with her arms on the fence rails.

"The Schoolteacher Answers the Call"

Evelyn Woodman was the teacher at the Malaga School from 1908 to 1911. Living in a small room attached to the schoolhouse, she provided year-round instruction in arithmetic, reading, the Bible, and domestic sciences.

The construction of the schoolhouse in 1908, which was paid for by private donations, was in large part the work of Captain George and Lucy Lane, missionaries from Malden, Massachusetts, who, along with their daughter Cora, first began visiting the island during the summer of 1906. I was able to read some of Evelyn Woodman's correspondence with Mrs. Lane at the Phippsburg Library, and this poem quotes some of that text directly.

"No Man's Land"

On the morning of July 14, 1911, Governor Plaistead, along with his Executive Council, made an official visit to inspect the conditions on Malaga Island. As recorded by the *Brunswick Times Record*, July 21, 1911, it was during this visit that Governor Plaistead declared: "The best plan would be to burn down the shacks with all their filth. Certainly the conditions are not creditable to our state, and we ought not to have such things near our front door, and I do not think that a like condition can be found in Maine, although there are some pretty bad localities elsewhere." This poem imagines the event as told through the eyes of Frances Gullifer, Governor Plaistead's wife.

"John Eason Stops Preaching"

Deacon John Eason was a carpenter, mason, and preacher. He was married to Rosilla Eason. The March 9, 2012, issue of the *Bath Independent* published a report, presented by another islander, Nelson McKenny, claiming that "Deacon John Eason has given up preaching and prayer-meeting through the troubles on his mind of leaving his old home and seeing all the old folks go too."

"What William Marks Knows, Age 3"

William Marks was the three-year-old son of Lizzie Marks. Because the Maine School for the Feeble- Minded housed male and female inmates in separate dormitories, he was separated from his mother upon admittance. He died at the Maine School for the Feeble-Minded in 1928.

"The Procedure"

This poem describes a sterilization procedure as imagined through the voice of Lizzie Marks. This is a liberty, as Lizzie Marks died in 1921, and sterilizations were not instituted at the Maine School for the Feeble-Minded until 1925. However, from 1925 through 1936, a total of at least 326 individuals underwent such procedures.

"Feeble-Minded"

This poem is written in the voice of Abbie Marks, who was one of the nine islanders remanded to the Maine School for the Feeble-Minded. It is addressed to her daughters, Lizzie, Lottie, and Etta, who were committed with her.

"Lottie Marks on Silence"

Lottie Marks died in July 1997 at the age of 103. Of the nine Malaga Island residents committed to the Maine School for the Feeble-Minded, Lottie and Abbie were the only ones ever released.

"Yellow Surprise"

The title and final line of this poem are taken from the final line of Richard Wright's "Between the World and Me."

"Shed Night"

This poem is for Gloria Harrison, daughter of Harold Tripp, and is based on an interview recording that was included in the Maine State Museum's 2012 exhibit, *Malaga Island, Fragmented Lives*, in which she recounts how her father's experience of childhood trauma affected her and her siblings. I had the pleasure of meeting Gloria Harrison and her family in July 2017 at a ceremony marking the placement of a new memorial in the New Gloucester cemetery honoring the Malaga Island residents who died at the Maine School for the Feeble-Minded, as well as those islanders whose graves were exhumed and reinterred there.

"Potter's Field" and "Paddling the Storm"

Unable to find a location where they were welcome to relocate, Robert and Laura Darling Tripp—along with their four children, Abbie, Leonard, Pearl, and Harold—lashed their home to a raft as a houseboat in order to float between neighboring islands. In November 1912, Laura Tripp became gravely ill in the middle of a severe storm. Robert Tripp rowed through the storm for a doctor but returned too late. Laura had already died, and it is said that her grieving children had to be pried from her body. These two poems attempt to tell this story through Harold's and Robert's eyes, respectively.

"Erasure"

This poem is an erasure using the original text of Holman Day's article, "The Queer Folk of the Maine Coast," originally published in the September 1909 issue of *Harper's Magazine*.

Acknowledgments

I am grateful to the editors of the following journals in which these poems first appeared, sometimes in earlier versions:

Bayou: "Dear ghosts, because you are dead and restless"
Bear Review: "Midden"
Border Crossing: "I Walk My Road at Dusk"
Grist Online: "Interview with the Dead"; *"The Tray of Spades"*; "Feeble Minded"; "Shed Night"; "Each Morning Drowns in Open Air"
The Maine Review: "The Story of Fire"; "Sucker Fish"; "Upon Opening Another Folded Day"
Sugar House Review: "The Way Home"; "Paddling the Storm"
White Stag Journal: "Dear ghosts, because you tell me to, I begin again"; "Dear ghosts, I wake wishing my body"; "Dear ghosts, I pick the list"; "Dear ghosts, how can we stop the sunlight from spinning the story"; "Dear ghosts, you say all our bones are made of paper"

Thank you to the Virginia Center for the Creative Arts and the Vermont Studio Center for residencies during which much of this work was written.

I am indebted to Bowdoin College Library's Special Collections, Burke Long, Kate McBrien of the Maine Historical Society, Maine State Archives, Tom Blake and Linda Gard of the New Gloucester Historical Society, and Peter Roberts for answering my many questions and for their assistance in locating the images that appear in the book.

Image citations and permissions are, in order of appearance, as follows:

Map of Casco Bay Maine, History of Lane's School on Malaga Island, p. 26, Mss A 1900, R. Stanton Avery Special Collections, reprinted with permission of the New England Historic Genealogical Society.

The 1907 Boston Post-Card Co.'s *The Tray of Spades* postcard has been reprinted with permission from the Bowdoin College Library's Special Collections.

The image of beds in New Gloucester Hall, Maine School for the Feeble-Minded, has been reprinted with permission by the New Gloucester Historical Society.

The document "Suggestions Made by Agent Pease" was provided by the Maine State Archives. The reprinted page is page five of a six-page document titled "Conditions at Malaga Island," Executive Council records, item #133.

The photograph of the east side of Malaga with "King Murphy" in his boat and the Phippsburg mainland in the background is courtesy of Peter Roberts.

I am deeply grateful to Daniel Midden for allowing his exquisite piece, "The Navigation of Bones" (red dress girl), 2012—part of his own series of work honoring the history of Malaga Island—to grace the cover of this book. Thank you, too, for your careful consideration of this project and for the powerful conversation we shared over coffee.

Thank you to those who carefully read drafts of this work, sometimes in its earliest forms, and provided guidance and support as the poems grew: Sara Borjas, Leonie Fogle, Frank Giampietro, Aracelis Girmay, Hope Jordan, Laura McCullough, Patricia Smith, Katharine Whitcomb, and Meg Willing.

Thank you to Afaa M. Weaver, to Elisabeth Frost, and to everyone at Fordham University Press. You have helped to usher this book into the world with love and care.

Thank you to my friends and family who have supported me in so many different ways throughout this process, especially my mother and sister, my partner, Walker, and his father, Michael Rothschild, who first planted the seed of this book in my head.

And to the descendants of Malaga Island, thank you, from the bottom of my heart—for breaking generations of silence and shame and for telling your stories. This book could not exist without you.

Peter Streckfus

Errings

Amy Sara Carroll

Fannie + Freddie: The Sentimentality of Post–9/11 Pornography

Nicolas Hundley

The Revolver in the Hive

Julie Choffel

The Hello Delay

Michelle Naka Pierce

Continuous Frieze Bordering Red

Leslie C. Chang

Things That No Longer Delight Me

Amy Catanzano

Multiversal

Darcie Dennigan

Corinna A-Maying the Apocalypse

Karin Gottshall

Crocus

Jean Gallagher
This Minute

Lee Robinson
Hearsay

Janet Kaplan
The Glazier's Country

Robert Thomas
Door to Door

Julie Sheehan
Thaw

Jennifer Clarvoe
Invisible Tender